Copyright © 2020 Clifton Townes
All rights reserved.
ISBN: 9798627981116

DEDICATION

All rights reserved. Neither this book nor any portion thereof may be reproduced or used in any manner whatsoever without the express written permission.

Disclaimer: The following book is for entertainment and informational purposes only. The information presented is without contract or any type of guarantee assurance. While every caution has been taken to provide accurate and current information, it is solely the reader's responsibility to check all information contained in this article before relying upon it. Neither the author nor publisher can be held accountable for any errors or omissions. Under no circumstances will any legal responsibility or blame be held against the author or publisher for any reparation, damages, or monetary loss due to the information presented, either directly or indirectly. This book is not intended as legal or medical advice. If any such specialized advice is needed, seek a qualified individual for help.

Trademarks are used without permission. Use of the trademark is not authorized by, associated with, or sponsored by the trademark owners. All trademarks and brands used within this book are used with no intent to infringe on the trademark owners and only used for clarifying purposes.

We hope you enjoy the St. Louis Blues Trivia Quiz Book.

CONTENTS

QUIZ 1 4

QUIZ 2 6

QUIZ 3 8

QUIZ 4 10

QUIZ 5 12

QUIZ 6 14

QUIZ 7 16

QUIZ 8 18

QUIZ 9 20

QUIZ 10 22

QUIZ 11 24

QUIZ 1

1. What Blues player was in the movie "Forrest Gump"?

2. What is the oldest arena that the Blues played in called?

3. What uniform number did Dale Hawerchuk initially wear when he played with the Blues in the 1995-96 season?

4. Glenn Hall was the first Blues starting goalie. Who was his back-up in their first season?

5. Here's an easy one: What player led the Blues in scoring (points) in the 92-93 season?

6. Who scored the first goal for the Blues?

7. In which year did the Blues start play?

8. What Blues player scored the Blues' first hat trick?

ANSWERS QUIZ 1

1. Brendan Shanahan

2. The Arena

3. 12

4. Seth Martin

5. Craig Janney

6. Larry Keenan

7. 1967

8. Camille Henry

QUIZ 2

1. Who was the first team that the St. Louis Blues competed against in the NHL?

2. Which one of these Blues players wore a uniform number in the sixties (between 60 and 69)?

3. Which of the following Blues jersey numbers have not been retired?

4. Who was the first head coach of the St. Louis Blues?

5. What team did the Blues hire coach Joel Quenneville away from?

6. Who was the Blues first owner?

7. Who had the Blues' first game miscconduct penalty?

8. How many seasons did Bernie Federko, who retired as the most prolific scorer in Blues history, play with the St. Louis Blues?

ANSWERS QUIZ 2

1. Minnesota North Stars

2. Pat Hickey

3. 7

4. Lynn Patrick

5. Colorado Avalanche

6. Sid Salomon Jr

7. Bob Plager

8. 13

QUIZ 3

1. What number did goalie Jim Carey wear as a member of the Blues?

2. Against what team did Red Berenson score 6 goals on November 7th, 1968?

3. Who is the only player to wear number 13?

4. What country is Roman Turek from?

5. In their short history, how many times have the Blues missed the playoffs?

6. Who was the first player to score 50 goals in a season?

7. What year did the Blues first start playing in the Kiel Center, which in 2003, was reanmedthe Savvis Center?

8. What number did Petr Nedved wear with the Blues in 1994?

ANSWERS QUIZ 3

1. 35

2. Philadelphia Flyers

3. Yuri Khmylev

4. Czechoslovakia

5. 3

6. Wayne Babych

7. 1994

8. 93

QUIZ 4

1. Who was the first Blue to win the Conn Smythe trophy as a member of the Blues?

2. Who holds the Blues record for most penalty minutes in one season?

3. Who scored 6 goals in one game for the Blues?

4. Who is Number 3 for the Blues retired for?

5. Who took the Blues' first penalty shot in history?

6. The first home game in 1994 in the new Kiel Center was played against what long rival team?

7. Which number did David Roberts not wear while a member of the Blues?

8. From which team did the Blues acquire Chris Pronger?

ANSWERS QUIZ 4

1. Glenn Hall

2. Bob Gassoff

3. Red Berenson

4. Bob Gassoff

5. Jim Roberts

6. LA Kings

7. 40

8. Hartford Whalers

QUIZ 5

1. Who was the first player taken by the Blues in the 93 draft?

2. Which player played in the Monday Night Miracle game?

3. What did Blues goalie Glenn Hall do before almost every game?

4. How many players wore the number 8, after Barclay Plager, before it was retired in 1980?

5. In 1991, _____ took his skills to comic book pages and became a superhero.

6. Which Blues player did not wear at least two different uniform numbers as a member of the Blues?

7. To what city did the Blues almost move?

8. Who led the Blues in penalty minutes in the 92-93 season?

ANSWERS QUIZ 5

1. Maxim Bets

2. Al MacInnis

3. Throw up

4. 4

5. Brett Hull

6. Adam Oates

7. Saskatoon

8. Garth Butcher

QUIZ 6

1. What Team did the Blues get Pavol Demitra from?

2. How many Stanley Cup Finals have the Blues been in?

3. What was Al MacInnis's nickname?

4. What future Hall of Fame inductee became the St. Louis head coach in 1967?

5. Which player wore number 2 immediately before Al MacInnis?

6. What was the St. Louis Arena called when Ralston Purina owned the team?

7. Who wore number 16 before Brett Hull?

8. How many team points did the Blues have in 1999-2000?

ANSWERS QUIZ 6

1. Ottawa Senators

2. 3

3. Chopper

4. Scotty Bowman

5. Curt Giles

6. Checkerdome

7. Jocelyn Lemieux

8. 114

QUIZ 7

1. How many total games have the Blues won in the Stanley Cup Finals?

2. What year was the Arena built and tore down?

3. Shayne Corson has worn number 27 for most of his career, but what number did he wear as a member of the Blues?

4. The Blues won what major team trophy in 1999-2000?

5. Which of the following goalies was NOT on the team in the 98-99 season?

6. What team did the Blues obtain Wayne Gretzky from?

7. Who did the Blues trade to obtain Chris Pronger?

8. What player was the last player to wear the number 36?

ANSWERS QUIZ 7

1. 0

2. 1929 &1999

3. 9

4. President's Trophy

5. Bruce Racine

6. Kings

7. Brendan Shanahan

8. Dan Trebil

QUIZ 8

1. Who was the last player to wear number 8 before it was retired in honor of Barclay Plager in 1982?

2. Which of the following has NOT been a coach of the Blues?

3. Who did the Blues receive from Detroit when they traded Vincent Riendeau?

4. What goalie holds the Blues record for wins?

5. Which division did the Blues once play in?

6. Who wore the number 24 before Bernie Federko?

7. What number did Harold Snepsts wear in his last game with the Blues?

8. What NHL team first competed in St. Louis as the Eagles?

ANSWERS QUIZ 8

1. Rick Bowness

2. Bob Hartley

3. Rick Zombo

4. Mike Liut

5. Norris

6. Doug Palazzari

7. 27

8. Ottawa Senators

QUIZ 9

1. What team did Reid Simpson begin his NHL career with?

2. Which of these Blues players never scored 50 or more goals?

3. Who scored the winning goal in the Blues Monday Night Miracle?

4. How many games did Wayne Gretzky play with the Blues, playoffs included?

5. What team did Jeff Finley begin his NHL career with?

6. Who did the Blues trade for Mike Eastwood?

7. Before coming to the NHL in 1967 as the St. Louis Blues, the St. Louis city had a team that only lasted one year in the NHL in 1934. What was their name?

8. Who was the first Blues player to wear number 3?

ANSWERS QUIZ 9

1. Philadelphia

2. Joey Mullen

3. Doug Wickenheiser

4. 31

5. NY Islanders

6. Harry York

7. The St. Louis Eagles

8. Al Arbour

QUIZ 10

1. While playing for the Blues, Gary Unger set the record for most consecutive games played, and never missed a game for the team. How many was it?

2. Who has scored the most short handed goals in Blues history?

3. What goalie in Blues history has played the most playoff games?

4. What ended Tony Twist's Career?

5. Who coached the Blues after Keenan was dumped?

6. Keith Tkachuk wore #7 on his jersey. Who wore it first for the Blues?

7. How many different players played for the Blues in the 95-96 season?

8. In the 1971-72 season, how many players on the Blues team had the last name of Plager?

ANSWERS QUIZ 10

1. 914

2. Larry Patey

3. Mike Liut

4. Motorcycle accident

5. Jimmy Roberts

6. Red Berenson

7. 49

8. 3

QUIZ 11

1. What Hall of Famer did the Blues sign in the 93-94 season?

2. With the addition of Chris Osgood to the Blues in the 2002-2003 season, how many Blues goaltenders will have started a game in 2003?

3. Which Blues player's wife did Brendan Shanahan have an affair with?

4. Who has been the St. Louis Blues head coach since January 6th, 1997, to 2003?

5. Which of the following is not a part of the 'Russian Experiment' the Blues tried in the 92 draft?

ANSWERS QUIZ 11

1. Peter Stastny

2. 7

3. Craig Janney

4. Joel Quenneville

5. Konstantin Shafranov

Made in the USA
Monee, IL
21 December 2022

23016485R00015